Threatened Cultures

BEDOUIN

John King

RSVP

RAINTREE
STECK-VAUGHN
P U B L I S H E R S
The Steck-Vaughn Company

Austin, Texas

Titles in the Series

Australian Aborigines
Bedouin
Inuit
Rain Forest Amerindians

Series editor: Paul Mason
Editor: Margot Richardson
Designer: Kudos Editorial and Design Services

Picture acknowledgments
The artwork on page 5 was supplied by Peter Bull.
The publishers gratefully acknowledge the permission of the following to
use their pictures: Associated Press/Topham 27 (top); Eye Ubiquitous 16
(bottom), 25, 41 (top); The Hutchison Library cover, 4 (left), 5, 11, 19 (top),
20, 21 (bottom), 26, 28, 30 (2), 31, 32, 33, 34, 35, 38, 39, 40, 41 (bottom), 43, 44;
Christine Osborne Pictures 4 (right), 6, 8, 9, 10 (2), 12, 13, 14, 15, 16 (top),
17, 18, 19 (bottom), 21 (top), 22, 23, 24, 27 (bottom), 29, 36, 37, 42, 45;
Laura Zito 7.

Library of Congress Cataloging-in-Publication Data
King, John, 1939-
    Bedouin / written by John King.
      p.   cm. — (Threatened cultures)
    Includes bibliographical references (p.   ) and index.
    Summary: Describes the Bedouin way of life as it has survived for
centuries in the Arab world and discusses threats to the continued
existence of this nomadic people's culture.
    ISBN 0-8114-2304-2
    1. Bedouins — Juvenile literature.   2. Arab countries —
Social life and customs — Juvenile literature.
[1. Bedouins.   2. Arab countries — Social life and customs.]
I. Title. II. Series.
DS36.9.B4K56 1993
961'.004933—dc20   92-16506
                         CIP AC

Printed by Lego, Italy
Bound in the United States by Lake Book, Melrose Park, IL

1 2 3 4 5 6 7 8 9 0 LB 98 97 96 95 94 93

Contents

Mansour and Selwa

In the southern part of Tunisia, Bedouin families still live on the edge of the desert, in the old way. Mansour and Selwa are two people who married when Mansour was twenty-two and Selwa was nineteen. They live with Mansour's family in its tents. The marriage of the two young people was arranged by their families. Mansour made a gift of money to Selwa's father, as well as giving money to Selwa herself which she spent on gold jewelry.

▲ A bride going to her wedding in traditional style, in Tunisia.

Mansour and Selwa's wedding was an important day. Selwa traveled to the wedding from where her own family lives. She made the journey in a special tent, riding on the back of a camel, while all her family rode or walked along with her. The men played music and sang and the women cried out in the particular Arab way known as ululation. The wedding was a ceremony that took part of its character from

▲ A Bedouin family and its camels on the move across the desert.

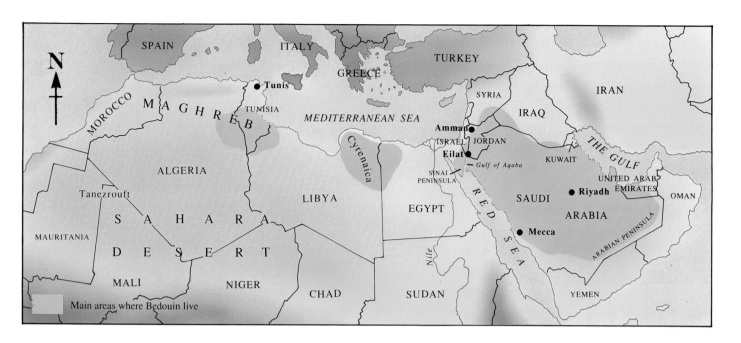

▲ The Bedouin can be found from Morocco in the west of northern Africa to the United Arab Emirates in the northeast of the Arabian Peninsula.

▲ Bedouin women spinning wool to be woven into tents or blankets.

Bedouin tradition and part from the Bedouin's Muslim religion.

The two families feasted together, the women with the women and the men with the men. Everyone wore their best clothes. The women's clothes were brightly colored, with long dresses, cloaks, and headscarves, and gold and silver jewelry. The men wore robes in white, brown, gray, and blue, with white turbans bound around their heads.

The dancing and singing went on all night after the wedding ceremony was over. But in the morning Selwa's family left for home, and Mansour and Selwa settled down to begin their life together. Mansour's father, Sheikh Hamid, was the leader of a group of Bedouin called the Hammama. Mansour's uncles and cousins and their wives and children also lived in the camp.

Everybody worked in the camp. There were many jobs, but the men herded the animals, went on any necessary journeys and errands, and stood guard; the women cooked and cleaned, took care of the poultry, and wove cloth and carpets. The children did not go to school and therefore could only learn to read if there was someone in the camp who could teach them. In the Hammama camp Sheikh Hamid taught the boys to read and recite the Koran. Fifteen people lived together in the camp, and all of them were related to each other.

The Hammama often stayed in one place for a long time, even for several years. They moved the tents whenever they needed to look for better grazing or to find better conditions.

▲ Bedouin from the Gulf region dancing at a festival, or "eid."

▲ Bedouin girls weaving on a wooden loom. The women enjoy weaving and take pride in the woven goods they produce.

But Tunisia is a small country, and the Hammama in the south seldom traveled more than a few hundred miles.

The Hammama family group lived by raising livestock. From their goats they got milk. The sheep provided the wool for the carpets and blankets that the women made on the wooden looms kept in the women's part of the tent. Meat came from the male kids and lambs. Hens gave eggs and meat. Donkeys and camels were used as beasts of burden, to carry loads.

Occasionally, the Hammama men made money by buying and selling camels. They also sometimes sold young goats and lambs for money to the farmers or people nearby, and they sold the carpets and blankets that the women made to a trader who came from the town, 30 miles away. The trader always tried to buy the blankets and carpets as cheaply as possible. The men negotiated prices, and the women were sometimes not pleased to see their work being sold too cheaply. They had worked hard to make the carpets and blankets the trader bought. All the money the family made was used in common, and everyone had ideas about how to spend it. The men had the final decision, but they listened to what the women said.

With the money, the Hammama bought the things they could not make themselves. They bought grain to make bread, coffee to drink, and

7

dates and honey to eat from the small farms at the oases and on the edge of the desert. From traders, they also bought cloth and other manufactured goods like knives and cooking pots. All the Bedouin families' possessions were stored in the women's side of the tents, for safety.

The government left the Hammama alone most of the time. They handled little money by the standards of the town, and so paid no taxes.

The Sahel

The area where the Hammama lived in southern Tunisia, known as the Sahel, is barren but beautiful. Rocks and hillsides contrast with the desert that stretches to the horizon. It is quiet and empty. But there is some water to be found and a little grazing for the flocks of hardy desert sheep and goats.

There was a government veterinarian, who helped with the animals if they were ill, but he was too busy to help much. Sometimes a government inspector or a policeman called at the camp. But the Hammama had little contact with the government and did not know much about their country's capital city, Tunis.

The Bedouin's homes were tents made of wool and goat hair and dyed black. The women wove the cloth from which the tents were made and helped to put them up and take them down when they were moved. The tents were low and wide and were propped up on tent poles. The tent was closed at the back, and at the front was a little space surrounded by thorn bushes weighted down with stones. The women's side of the tent, where the women and children lived, was divided from the men's side by an interior

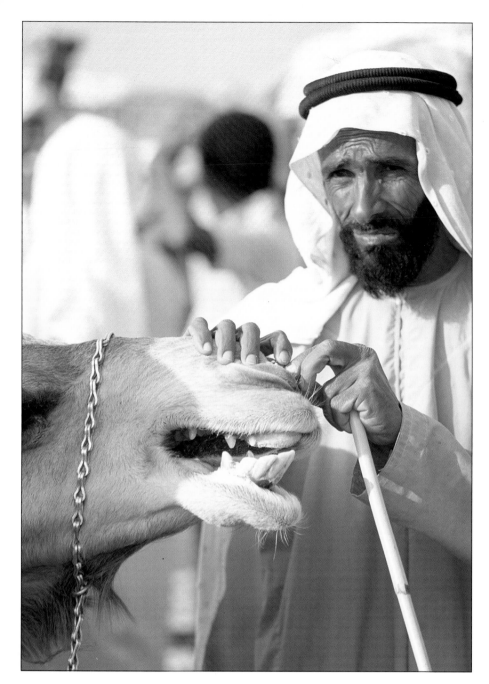

A camel trader. Camels have always been important for transportation in the desert, because they are able to exist for long periods without much water.

wall of fabric. There were several tents in the camp, where the different families lived. The animals grazed near the tents.

The Hammama worked hard from early in the morning until dark. But in the evening the men sat together while the women served their evening meal, and both the men and the women sat and ate. The children played games that they had learned from their older brothers and sisters. Their toys were the sticks and stones they found around the camp. They sang songs and rhymes and played the same games that their mothers and fathers had when they were children. The older people liked to listen to Sheikh Hamid telling stories about what the Bedouin did hundreds of years ago. They were very proud of being Bedouin themselves. As the camp fire burned, the Hammama ate, gossiped, and talked business.

At first, Mansour and Selwa settled in to live with the rest of the family group. Selwa helped to make the carpets that the family sold and did

9

her part of the cooking and the jobs the women did, like scouring cooking pots and collecting eggs. Mansour worked as a shepherd, as he had done since he was a little boy. He was the strongest man in the camp, and his work was important to the group.

Life was hard for the Hammama and was becoming harder. There had not been enough rain for many years on the fringe of the desert. That meant that there was less and less grazing for the sheep and goats, and water was hard to find. The Bedouin had less to sell, and so it was harder to make a living. Sometimes the farmers lent them money to tide them over in bad times, but money was scarce. Their reserves of food for themselves and their animals were

▲ A very old camel saddlebag, which a bride would take to her new home.

▲ Bedouin women, in brightly colored clothes, visit a market to buy food they cannot produce themselves.

falling low, and the older men worried about how they would cope in the future.

After a year of marriage, Mansour and Selwa had a son. There was much rejoicing among the tents, and the women in particular made a great fuss over Selwa and the new baby. But Mansour decided that the time had come for him to leave the family group and to go abroad to earn some money. Selwa was sad, but of course she could go on living with the family. Sheikh Hamid treated Selwa like his own daughter, and she could bring up her baby with the other children.

Mansour made the journey to Tunis, where he found a boat to take him to Italy, to get a job working on a farm. A year later he came home, with money and presents for his wife, his father, and his family. The money made life easier for the Hammama, and Mansour worked with his father, his uncles, and his brothers as before, with the flocks of sheep and goats. He brought ornaments for the women, toys for the children, and best of all a television set, with batteries to make it work. But, in the end, the family did not like the television. Both the men and the women

A young girl in her best clothes, in front of a Bedouin woven rug. ▶

were shocked and embarrassed by some of the programs, and they would rather listen to Sheikh Hamid's stories.

Soon after Mansour's return there was a disaster for the family. One day, two policemen came to take photographs of each person in the family group, and to ask for their names and dates of birth, so that they could have government identity cards. The policemen were disrespectful to the Bedouin, because they thought they were simple country people. The women were especially embarrassed to have their photographs taken because it was Hammama custom for women to veil their faces when there were strangers present. When the policemen took Mansour's details, they discovered that he had never served in the army. Sheikh Hamid explained that the family depended on Mansour and on the money he could bring back from abroad. But the police came back and took Mansour away to join the army for two years, as all young men must do in Tunisia.

Without Mansour, and with no more money to come from abroad, the Hammama men decided that they could not continue their way of life in the desert. Sheikh Hamid was very sad to have to change, but the younger men persuaded him. When an important decision like this was made, the men made the choice, but the women all said what they thought. The Hammama moved north, to find a place where there was more water and more for the sheep and goats to eat. Some of the men now had to take jobs on farms instead of working for

▲ Bedouin women, keeping their faces covered in the presence of strangers, peek out from their tent made of camel and goat hair.

themselves. Some of them even went into the towns to find work there.

When Mansour came home from his military service, he found that the camp where he grew up had gone and his family was broken up, with his brothers and uncles scattered to different places. Perhaps he would live with Selwa and his little son on a farm where he could work for wages. Or he might go into the town to get a job, perhaps as a laborer or in a factory. But for Mansour and Selwa the Bedouin way of life had come to an end.

The government in Tunisia knows that it is hard for the Bedouin to continue in modern times. It believes it can help the Bedouin have a better life, with more money, and with doctors

Ancestors

The people who live in the towns and on the farms are sad to see the Bedouin giving up their old ways. Arab people know that their ancestors were once Bedouin, and they like to see the tents, the sheep, and the camels. The townspeople know that all the oldest Arab stories are about Bedouin who lived in tents just like their descendants do today. On the other hand, some townspeople believe the Bedouin are dishonest or look down on the Bedouin because of their simple ways.

to look after the Bedouin men and women and schools for the Bedouin children. But that would be easier if the Bedouin would settle down in villages. There are fewer and fewer Bedouin families like the Hammama keeping up the old traditions on the edge of the desert, and one day there may be no more.

A Time of Troubles

Mansour and Selwa are part of the new generation of Bedouin people in Tunisia. As we found out from their story, it is hard for them to go on making a living in the traditional way. But why is that so? What is different now? And why do young Bedouin today face problems that older generations did not?

The Bedouin are Muslims in their religion and speak the Arabic language, like their neighbors. But their problems are special to them and come from their way of life. In many ways the Bedouin men, women, and children are very different from the settled people around them, and they are very proud of their customs and their individuality.

DRIER CLIMATE

First of all, a family of Bedouin depends on its animals to live. Everything that both the men and the women do is based on what they

▲ Sheep and goats, the Bedouin's most important possessions, drink from a well in the desert.

▲ An oasis spring provides water for herds of camels.

can get from their camels, sheep, and other livestock. Wool, meat, milk, eggs, and leather all come from the animals. However, relying on them has become harder to do. Since 1980, the Bedouin have had bad years because the weather has become steadily drier, and so the land on the fringes of the desert has become more arid. As the underground aquifers have dried up, there has been less water and less grazing for the sheep and goats.

Water is a vital element in Bedouin life wherever the Bedouin make their homes. When the men are deciding where they should move the camp, they search for a place where the women and children will be comfortable. They avoid the driest part of the desert, where there is no water at all. They always look for places where there may be water sources. At the oases, which indicate springs in the desert where underground water comes to the surface, the Bedouin pass by to trade and talk to the settled people. The parts of the desert where the Bedouin live may look inhospitable, but there is always some sparse vegetation. A Bedouin proverb says, "Water is the Sultan's friend."

TRADING FOR FOOD

At the same time the farmers in the oases, where the Bedouin obtain food in exchange for meat and milk, have also had to struggle. Their crops have been less plentiful due to the drier climate, leaving them less food to sell. The farmers have had to charge more for what they grow to try to make

West have had unemployment and sharply rising prices. There has been less money for governments and people to spend. That means that Europe buys less from Tunisia and other so-called developing countries, so there is less money for Tunisians to spend. In the end, all this means that less money finds its way to the Bedouin.

At the same time, people from the West have less to spend on vacations so fewer people come to Tunisia. And since 1990 there has been another problem. After the crisis that led to the Gulf War

▲ Police in Jordan use camels to patrol the desert regions.

enough money to support themselves and their families.

The Bedouin have not been able to maintain the emergency stores of grain and animal feed that the women keep in big storage baskets in the camp. These are the supplies used for food when times are bad, to tide the Bedouin family over when they cannot find or buy anything to eat. And at the same time, the shepherds and their flocks have had to range wider and wider each day in order to find enough grazing, while at home the women and children wait anxiously for their return.

The Bedouin's other way of trading is by selling the woven goods the women make. Traders, like the one who came to the Hammama camp, try to buy the blankets and carpets as cheaply as they can. They then bring a good price in the shops in Tunis and the other towns, where wealthier Tunisians and tourists from Europe buy them. But it is vital for the Bedouin people to get a good price for the carpets and blankets when they are sold to traders. That is becoming more difficult.

This is because around the world in the 1980s and 1990s there have been economic problems. All the countries in Europe and elsewhere in the

Weaving

Bedouin blankets and carpets are very well made and beautiful to look at. The women have great skill in weaving on the wooden looms, which are precious and are passed down in families from mothers to daughters. The blankets and carpets take a long time to make. The women enjoy making them, and there is a lot of singing and talking while they work.

▲ Bedouin use camels, horses, and donkeys as forms of transportation and often visit nearby oases to buy food.

with Iraq, very few people from Europe and the U.S. traveled to the Arab world. Even though the Gulf Crisis is now over, there are still few Western tourists in Arab countries. In Tunisia, that means there is less demand for the Bedouin carpets, and the price falls.

WORKING ABROAD

In the Hammama camp, Mansour made his own decision about what to do about the tough conditions that his wife, his baby son, and his elderly father were facing. He did what many young Tunisian men do and went abroad in search of work. Young non–Bedouin men from the towns and villages also go abroad, because there is high unemployment in Tunisia. Half the people in Tunisia are less than twenty–five years old, so there are many young men looking for work.

From families like Mansour's, only the young men go abroad. The older men and the women stay at home in the Bedouin camps. In the past, it has been easy for a young Tunisian to find work in Italy, although it became harder during the 1980s and 1990s as there was less money in the West to employ foreign workers. The young Tunisians often work without proper permission from the Italian government, and they are paid low wages.

In Italy, their life is hard, and the workers often sleep in huts and tents among the fields. But the Bedouin are used to conditions like that. And, by the standards of the Tunisian workers, the wages seem high. When they take their Italian money home to Tunisia they seem like wealthy men. Nevertheless, they are still very glad to come home, to find their wives and children waiting for them. It is sad when a young man has to work abroad and does not see his children growing up.

THE GOVERNMENT

The Bedouin in Tunisia have always wanted to have as little as possible to do with the government. They pay no taxes, because they do not use much money in their way of life, and because it is difficult to measure their income. Sometimes they come into contact with police patrols, or with border guards in the parts of Tunisia near the Algerian and Libyan frontiers. However, there are government officials whose job it is to keep an eye on life in the desert, and social workers try to make some contact with the Bedouin, especially to look after the welfare of the women and the children living in the harsh desert conditions. And there is some practical help from the government for the

▲ Desert life is hard for women. There is little water; it can be very hot during the day, yet freezing at night.

Bedouin men, like the veterinary service provided by the Tunisian Ministry of Agriculture that helps to keep flocks of sheep and herds of camels in a healthy condition.

The government wants to register all Tunisia's citizens and to issue them identity cards. That is regarded by the Bedouin as an invasion of their privacy. The men do not like photographs to be taken of the women, or for officials to know private details about them. And the women are often embarrassed by having to talk to strangers, because they have been brought up to speak freely only with members of their own families. The government also makes young men living in the Bedouin camps do their military service like other young men in Tunisia. Exceptions are sometimes made when a young man is the breadwinner for a family and their sole source of income. But most young Bedouin men must go into the army. That brings them into contact with the outside world and makes it more likely that they will later turn to a settled job on a farm or even in a town.

The tough conditions in the desert today are another reason the Bedouin are changing their way of life. They move north where there is more water and better grazing for the animals. That means life for the women and children is safer and less difficult. Moving north puts the Bedouin into contact with farmers. Sometimes the Bedouin men begin to work on farms for wages or even take jobs in the towns. The women stay at home, but if the men are earning more money they will often bring home food and clothing in a way that was not possible in the desert, and the women's old way of life begins to change.

LIVING IN TOWNS

This contact between Bedouin and townspeople can bring its own problems because the townspeople often do not understand the Bedouin. They have a romantic idea of the Bedouin,

▲ Oasis farming: plowing the land with a camel.

living in tents and roaming freely in the desert. At heart, many think the Bedouin life is the ideal of how an Arab person should live.

But when the Bedouin men come into the town, they sometimes look poor and dirty, and people fear that they will become thieves and live dishonestly. The townspeople and the police sometimes clash with the Bedouin, who find that they are being looked down on or even treated like criminals.

This means that the Bedouin must be taught town ways if they are to survive, while the townspeople need to learn how to treat the Bedouin with respect and to trust them. In the end, government officials often conclude that the best way to solve the problem of integrating the Bedouin into the national life of Tunisia is to settle them down and turn them into ordinary citizens as quickly as possible. This may end the Bedouin way of life in Tunisia.

▲ The bustling city of Tunis. Many Bedouin have never lived in cities or towns.

3 The Bedouin World

DESERT DWELLERS

There are Bedouin across the Arab world, from Morocco in the west to Oman in the east. Everywhere the Bedouin live, their lives and customs are similar. They roam freely in the deserts and pay little attention to the borders between countries. Even today they often tend to regard themselves as independent from governments and only have dealings with the authorities when they must.

One reason the Bedouin live in the same way, whatever country they are in, is that they always live in places that are alike in climate and landscape. The Bedouin live on the edge of the desert, in places where there is a little vegetation and some rain.

The places where Bedouin choose to live look very harsh to outsiders, but the Bedouin do not go into the heart of the desert. In the Empty Quarter, in the middle of the Arabian Peninsula, or the Tanezrouft at the heart of the Sahara desert, no life can survive for long.

▲ Water is scarce on the edges of the desert.

▲ The heart of the Sahara — too harsh even for the Bedouin.

All the Arab countries are on the edge of the desert, so virtually every Arab country has some areas of the kind the Bedouin prefer. In North Africa, or the Maghreb as the Arabs call it, the three countries of Tunisia, Algeria, and Morocco lie along the northern edge of the Sahara, between the desert and the sea.

Farther east, in Libya, the desert almost touches the coastline. In Egypt the country is virtually all desert except for the cultivated area of the Nile river delta and a ribbon of land by the Nile stretching from Upper Egypt down to the frontier with another desert country, Sudan.

Syria and Jordan lie on one edge of the Syrian Desert, with Iraq at its other edge. To the south, the Syrian Desert links up with the desert heart

▲ A Bedouin man and his sons kill a goat to provide meat for their family.

An oasis dweller climbs up a date palm to harvest the dates. He will then sell these to other people, including the Bedouin.

of Saudi Arabia, which occupies most of the Arabian Peninsula.

ECONOMY

In all these deserts there are Bedouin. And in all these countries the Bedouin live in a similar way, with their flocks of goats and sheep, their horses, donkeys, and camels, and their black woolen tents. From desert to desert the Bedouin economy is always the same. They sell the produce of their flocks: meat, milk, and wool, and the blankets and carpets made by the women. At the same time, they buy from the settled people on the edge of the desert the things they cannot make or grow themselves: manufactured goods, in addition to the grain and dates that form part of their staple diet.

Bedouin culture in each of these countries is essentially the same. Independence and a good reputation with their neighbors are the things Bedouin men value. A Bedouin woman likes to see her tents well run and the people well fed, with her children making good marriages. Among the Bedouin, weddings set up new families and bring the birth of children who will carry on the family name. Marriages also help to bring friendship and alliances between groups of neighboring Bedouin.

DIFFERENT TRIBES

The most famous Bedouin groups, or tribes, live in the east, in the Syrian Desert. These are called the Anazeh Bedouin, and while their numbers can only be guessed at, there are perhaps a million or so. Among the Anazeh, the largest tribe is the Rualla. The names of the Anazeh and the Rualla are mentioned in Arab manuscripts and by European travelers many centuries ago. There are about a quarter of a million Rualla Bedouin, who live by herding camels and sheep.

▲ Sheep are useful to the Bedouin, providing milk for food as well as wool for weaving cloth.

Bedouin women usually wear jewelry every day. The "hand" motif is believed to protect the wearer and is very common in northern Africa.

The Rualla live in a part of the Syrian Desert called the Great Nafud, between Syria, Iraq, and Saudi Arabia. They move into different parts of the desert at different times of the year, following the water supply and finding places where the climate suits their animals better. The Nafud covers about 200,000 square miles, and is about 450 miles wide. It is very hot in summer and often freezing in winter. Small groups of Rualla may be found anywhere from the east coast of the Arabian Peninsula in the United Arab Emirates (which is the southernmost extent of their territory) to the Syrian–Turkish border in the north.

In Egypt there are Bedouin in the Sinai Peninsula and in the Western Desert, between Egypt and Libya. In Egypt they are a small minority, but there are more Bedouin in Libya, especially in the eastern part of the country known as Cyrenaica.

In Tunisia, Mansour and Selwa's home, there is only a small minority of Bedouin, perhaps a few hundred thousand. In the Sahara desert as a whole, there may be several million nomadic people. These are Bedouin in the north, and Touareg farther south. They range over many countries, including Libya, Tunisia, Algeria, and Morocco to the north and Chad, Niger, and Mali to the south.

Every Arab country has its Bedouin, and in the heart of the Middle East, Israel also has a Bedouin population. The Negev desert in southern Israel is Bedouin country. It lies between the inhabited parts of the country in the north where most Israelis live and the port of Eilat on the Gulf of 'Aqaba to the south. Israel is a Jewish state, set up in 1948 by Jewish immigrants to Palestine, but it has an Arab minority. The Bedouin of the Negev are part of Israel's original Arab population.

Frontiers

Perhaps because they are used to traveling overland in difficult terrain, on horses and camels instead of on roads, the Bedouin men do not respect frontiers. Frontiers and other boundaries of settled life have little meaning in a traditional nomadic culture, such as the Bedouin's. Therefore, whether a member of the Rualla tribe is of Iraqi or Syrian nationality is not as important to the Bedouin as it is to settled people.

SIMILARITIES

All these Bedouin people have many features of their way of life in common, especially their reliance on their flocks and herds. Both men and women share many customs and habits, and Bedouin folktales and folk songs have common strains from one country to another. The family life of the Bedouin is similar across the whole Arab world. The men and women wear the same kind of clothes and the children play similar games. But of course they do differ in some ways, depending on where they live.

Local conditions have made a difference in the customs of the Bedouin, especially when they meet settled people in the towns. These people have different customs according to the different countries in which they live. But across the Arab world, the similarities between the Bedouin and the way they live are more marked than their differences.

Bedouin in Jordan

In Jordan, too, the Bedouin tribes are linked to the country's rulers. A family called the Hashemites, led by brothers Abdullah and Faisal, fought alongside Lawrence of Arabia against the Turks in World War I, and became kings in Iraq and Jordan. The men who fought with them were mainly Bedouin. The present king of Jordan, King Hussein (left), is descended from King Abdullah, one of the Hashemite family. King Hussein's favorite troops, which form his personal guard, are Bedouin. They wear the red and white Arab headdress with their uniforms.

▲ The landscape looks harsh to outsiders, but Bedouin have lived in areas like this in Israel for centuries.

How the Bedouin Live

▲ Although Bedouin like to keep camels, sheep are now profitable to raise.

We have learned about how the Hammama Bedouin of Tunisia make their living, and what their life is like. We have also seen how the Bedouin spread across the Arab world, wherever there is a desert. We shall look at how the Bedouin in two other parts of the Arab world live and at their relations with the government.

THE RUALLA

First we look at the Rualla Bedouin in Syria, mentioned in the last chapter. The Rualla are herdsmen, and in the past the animals they kept were camels. Today the Rualla have started keeping sheep. Camels are more expensive to buy and take longer to breed into a bigger herd. But the real problem with camels is that they are no longer needed for transportation. Few people want to ride camels or use them to carry loads when they can use trucks and jeeps instead.

That means there is no longer a market for camels to be used as beasts of burden. As producers of wool, meat, and milk, sheep are much more useful. The Rualla Bedouin still keep some camels, but this is partly just because they like camels more than sheep. Keeping camels is seen as a manly occupation for the Rualla men. Keeping sheep does not have the same dignity.

The Rualla are also great traders. They will buy and sell anything that is in demand. For example, a Rualla in another part of Saudi Arabia hears that there is a shortage of car tires in Riyadh, the capital, so he buys up a load of car tires and takes them to Riyadh to sell. Chopped straw for camel fodder is bought in Syria and sold in Saudi Arabia. Sheep are bought on the Turkish border and brought south.

In the past, the Rualla men have also been raiders and smugglers. Now, raiding other tribes or settled communities to steal goods and animals has virtually vanished. But smuggling was still a part of the Rualla's life in the 1980s, and some of it still goes on. Cars and goods like television sets and video recorders are moved about Syria and Saudi Arabia and across frontiers. In particular there was a demand in Syria for television sets bought cheaply in Saudi Arabia. After the Gulf War the Middle East's frontiers are more carefully guarded by military forces. Many of the chances to smuggle goods between countries have gone.

The Rualla Bedouin have also moved into employment. The oil industry has been a great employer of labor in the Middle East. Rualla have been trained in many technical jobs. But they seldom forget they are Bedouin. Their wages are often used for the support of families still herding camels. A man with a job will sometimes quit and go back to the desert for a while, before returning to his work as a plumber or an electrician. Here, as elsewhere in the Arab world, the Bedouin women do not seek jobs.

The Rualla men also take jobs in towns in different countries. One Rualla Bedouin who was the sheikh of a group based in northern Saudi Arabia some years ago had three brothers. One was working in Damascus, the capital of Syria; one was working in Amman, the capital of Jordan; and the third was in the U.S.

Rualla women do not work outside the tents

▲ Many Bedouin now have technical training and work in the Middle East's oil industry.

▲ A woman's prized gold jewelry always remains her own property.

Sheikhs

Politics among the Rualla is organized in a way unique to the Bedouin. The Rualla have their own sheikhs, or leaders, who have wide influence among the tribe. But they work through persuasion rather than force. The governments of the countries in which the Rualla live know that they have to deal with the sheikhs if they want to control the Bedouin.

or take much part in the tribe's public life. But they play a major part in family life, which is important to the Bedouin. When a Bedouin man marries a woman, he links himself with her family. A Bedouin woman has property of her own, in the form of clothes and gold jewelry, so that she always has some independence. The work in the camp is hard, but a woman's mother and aunts as well as her children will help her to run the tent. They bring wood, collect dried camel dung for the fire, and wash the clothes, as well as sew, bake, and help to put up the tents when necessary.

▲ Bedouin women do much of the work when putting up tents at a new camp.

◄ Special occasions, like the arrival of visitors or the birth of a new baby, are often celebrated with a feast.

The Rualla women regard as very important the way they help to link families together through their own marriages and help to arrange the marriages of their children. They are proud of their families and of their husbands' successes. A well-run and well-made tent is a source of prestige for a Bedouin family, together with the luxuries the women work hard to provide. The women are often very knowledgeable about the affairs of the Rualla and their neighbors, and will offer their opinions to the men.

Sometimes governments have tried to control the Bedouin. At one time, for example, the Rualla were smuggling such large amounts of American cigarettes into Syria that the Syrian government put many soldiers with guns and helicopters on the border to try to stop them. On another occasion, the Jordanian government tried to make the Bedouin get license plates for the trucks they use, but after a long argument they were allowed to continue using them in the desert with no license plates. In Saudi Arabia, the government built housing for the

▲   Many Bedouin in Israel have ceased to roam the desert and now live in houses.

Bedouin and offered them cash grants to help them live there.

But governments are sometimes helped by the Bedouin. King Hussein of Jordan was once threatened by some politicians and soldiers who wanted to take over the government and make him step down. A Bedouin chief and a thousand armed Bedouin on camels came to the Jordanian capital to help protect the king. Even in the modern world, the Rualla Bedouin still lead their own lives, to a great extent untouched by the government or by rules and regulations. They live according to their own rules and their own code of honor. But the changing world does have an effect on Bedouin society. The

Bedouin are now very much more aware of what happens in the world outside their desert pastures. And though they are threatened by it, they are often able to use it to their own advantage.

ISRAELI BEDOUIN

In Israel, the Bedouin of the Negev are a different case. Although Israel is a Jewish state, many Arabs still live within the frontiers. There are about 100,000 Bedouin in the Negev. One tribe there is called the Uqbi. Long ago, these Bedouin used to roam throughout the whole Negev, but by 1948, when the state of Israel was formed, they were already mostly small farmers.

The Israeli authorities have moved the Bedouin families to supervised areas, where they live with government permission. Israel plans that all the Bedouin will eventually live in new settlements especially set up for them. The Uqbi and the other tribes of the Negev have not lost their Bedouin traditions altogether, but even before the Israelis came, most of them no longer lived in the black wool tents but had moved to houses.

Everything the Bedouin do in the Negev is carefully controlled by the Israeli government. The Bedouin settlements are watched by Israeli border guards. If the Bedouin try to build houses anywhere other than the areas where they are permitted to live, even on land which was once theirs, the Israeli authorities demolish them. Farming by the Bedouin is strictly limited. There are limits on the amount of land they can use for grazing, and on the size of flocks of sheep and herds of goats they are permitted to have. And

Losing Their Home

This is how one Uqbi Bedouin in the Negev remembers what happened to his family.

"In 1948 when I was six my family was living in Beersheba, but our land was in Araqib nearby. My family was afraid to stay in the town so they left before the army came and went to Araqib, leaving most of their possessions behind them. My father told the Israelis: 'We want to live on our land and become citizens.' In 1951 one day some soldiers came early in the morning. They shot in the air to frighten us. They told my father we had to leave and go to another place. They put us in Hora. There was no water supply and no road for more than ten years."

they may not take more than a fixed amount of water from the wells.

More and more, the Bedouin men are becoming paid workers for Israeli employers. Israeli settlers in the Negev employ the Bedouin

▲ The water supply at a Bedouin settlement in Israel comes only from these tankers. Often, the amount of water they may use is strictly limited by the government.

as farm laborers. There is also building work to be done for the Israelis as they expand their own towns and settlements, as well as work on roads and irrigation projects.

In the Negev, as in the Syrian Desert, the women were vital to the economy. They cared for the flocks and herds, and milked the goats, sheep, and camels. They wove cloth and cooked, as well as sewed and mended, and brought in wood and water, just as the Rualla women do. But since 1948, the women have lost much of their status. In settled communities the work they do is less important, since their husbands bring home a wage and the family then buys the things it needs. Some women are being educated and a few work outside the home, unlike the vast majority of Bedouin women elsewhere. But most are caught in the trap of losing their traditional work in and around the Bedouin tents, while failing to find a new way of life.

Israel is developing the Negev, on the land that used to belong to the Bedouin. Farms and settlements are being built. The vacation resort and seaport of Eilat in the south is being built up. The town of Beersheba, at the northern edge of the desert, has industry and a university. And the center of Israel's nuclear industry, where there is a big nuclear reactor with factories and workshops, is at Dimona, in the heart of the old Bedouin lands in the Negev.

Like other Arabs who live inside Israel, the Bedouin are Israeli citizens. Some Bedouin

▲ With the move from tents to houses, and with many Bedouin men taking paid work, the women's role in the family also often changes.

▲   The traditional way of life, including the way people dress, is disappearing for many Bedouin.

men even serve in the Israeli army, which Arab Israelis are not normally allowed to do. A survey that asked Bedouin in the Negev how they thought of themselves revealed that they said they were Palestinians, and that their nationality was Israeli. The old Bedouin life, with sheikhs who have influence, just as there are in the Rualla and other tribes in the Arab countries, is dying out. Young Bedouin often believe the sheikhs now just do what the Israeli government wants them to do.

In spite of their disadvantages, more young Bedouin men and some women are being educated in Israel, and some go on to college. They are beginning to think like the Arabs of Israel's towns, who have a difficult time adjusting to being citizens of the Jewish state. Arab countries are hostile to Israel, and the Israeli Arabs have a divided loyalty.

What is happening to the Bedouin in Israel shows what could happen to Bedouin everywhere if they are carefully controlled and if the right to move around in their land and graze their animals is taken away from them. They lose their special character. The young men and women become just like other young Arab men and women living on farms and in towns and villages, earning wages and buying what they need with money.

The Bedouin self-sufficiency disappears, and the Bedouin people disappear as they move out of the desert. The Bedouin way of life ceases to exist, as surely as if the people themselves were killed off.

5 The Bedouin in History

CAMEL NOMADS

Anthropologists call the Bedouin way of life "camel nomadism." This means that the Bedouin travel from place to place with their camels, which provide them with their livelihood. People like the Bedouin have been living this way for four thousand years. There were camel nomads in Arabia a thousand years before the earliest civilization in Greece, and two thousand years before the Roman Empire. People similar to the Bedouin in their way of life were living in the Arabian Desert when the pyramids were built in Egypt, and while the Bronze Age Celtic people flourished in Europe.

ISLAM

The earliest Arab camel nomads lived in the Arabian Peninsula, in the territory that is now Saudi Arabia. They spread through the Arab world with the expansion of Islam (the religion of Muslims) over 1,300 years ago, in A.D. 622, which is the date from which we count the beginning of the Islamic era.

In its first hundred years, Islam spread throughout the Middle East and then along the coast of North Africa, on the southern shore of the Mediterranean Sea. Bedouin tribesmen brought the new language, Arabic, and the new faith to all the lands that were to become Arab countries.

▲ Many Bedouin still use camels as their main form of transportation.

▲ It is not unusual to see the old and new ways of life combined. Some families make enough money from trading or working abroad to buy a jeep or truck for transportation.

CHANGES

It is very easy to make a mistake about people who in some ways resemble their ancestors who lived hundreds or thousands of years ago. When we meet the Bedouin today, we are not meeting people who think or act like people did thousands of years ago. Though they still ride their camels and graze their flocks, the modern Bedouin think and act in a different way.

People never stop changing. We do not live or talk the same way our mothers and fathers did. We are even more different from our grandfathers and grandmothers, and we can scarcely imagine what it was like before that. In the same way, our children will lead different lives, and their children will be more different still.

It is like that with the Bedouin. The modern Bedouin speak differently, think in a new way, and do not share the same ideas as their ancestors. When people are attempting to introduce a different way of doing something, they often try to show that people have done it that way in the past. If accepted, the new way becomes part of the "tradition." Modern Bedouin may follow the "old ways," but many traditions go back only a few generations.

So it is important to remember that today's Bedouin are modern men and women. They may share some practices and customs with their ancestors, but they are very different from them. In the same way, the modern Bedouin share many of the things they do with the other great group of camel nomads, the Touareg, but the Bedouin and the Touareg are very foreign to one another.

STORIES

The sense of history and the old stories are very important to the Bedouin and to all the Arabs. The Bedouin still tell old tales about their ancestors from long ago. In Tunisia, for example, the Bedouin tell the stories of the Beni Hilal, the tribe that brought the Arabic language and culture with them to the Maghreb from Arabia. And one of the best-known and most popular collections of stories in Arab literature are the tales of Antar and Abla, a Bedouin hero and heroine. Those stories were first written down, in the form we have them today, in the thirteenth century, seven hundred years ago.

Poetry and literature are important to the Bedouin and are part of their sense of history. Stories and poems are often handed down by word of mouth, without being written down. The Algerian hero, the Emir Abd al-Qadir, who fought against the French while they colonized Algeria in the nineteenth century, wrote a poem that the Bedouin tent is a house of wool ("sha'r" in Arabic), but it is also a house of poetry ("shi'r" in Arabic). Arab poets love a play on words of that kind, and the vocabulary of Arabic is very large and expressive.

INDEPENDENCE

In more recent times, we hear constantly of the Bedouin in historical documents. The Rualla of

▲ A Bedouin woman, living in a house in Israel, still makes flat bread in the traditional way, over an open fire.

Syria and Arabia, for example, are first mentioned three hundred years ago. Other Arabian tribes also belong to the great Anazeh confederation. As we have seen, they are very proud of not being obedient to any one country's government. But it is uncertain in modern times how truly independent the Bedouin can be. What is important is that the Bedouin themselves believe that they are independent.

A hundred years ago, the Rualla and other tribes were a constant problem for the Turkish Empire, known as the Ottoman Empire, which then ruled most of the Arab world. They raided the towns and farms on the edge of the desert when they chose to do so, and they sometimes plundered the caravans that took pilgrims across the desert to Mecca for the pilgrimage which all Muslims should make at least once in their lives. The local governors offered them gifts of money and animals in order to keep them away.

Even in the twentieth century, the Bedouin have sometimes been a problem for governments. Sometimes they have played an important role, for example, when the tribes fought with the British and French against the Turks and Germans in World War I and when the Bedouin helped Ibn Saud to found the Kingdom of Saudi Arabia.

MYTHOLOGY

On the other hand, the Bedouin provide a mythology for Arab people and Arab governments to believe in. Many Arab townspeople dislike the Bedouin when they actually meet them. But they have a romantic idea of the Bedouin as having all the Arab virtues of generosity, steadfastness, and courage.

Arab rulers like King Hussein of Jordan and King Hassan of Morocco like to encourage the idea that their ancestors came out of the desert. The ruler of Libya, Colonel Qaddafi, who was born in a Bedouin tent in the Libyan desert, still likes to live in a tent. And at the summit

▲ Young Bedouin today may not be given the choice of following the same way of life as their parents and grandparents.

conference of the Arabian Gulf states, at the end of 1991, the ruler of Kuwait had a huge Bedouin tent made for the leaders to meet in.

The Bedouin are still most able to live the life they choose in the Great Nafud and the Syrian Desert. There, tribal structures still remain, and they can still graze camels, the animals closest to the Bedouin's heart. Where the Bedouin are more limited by government control and only a smaller space is available to them, like in Tunisia, their way of life is in danger. And in the Negev, where the Israeli government has almost completely

Men and women usually eat and drink separately from each other. ▶

◀ Most Israeli Bedouin have been forced to abandon their nomadic existence and live in villages or towns.

stopped them from leading their old life, they are becoming day by day more like the townspeople.

THE PEOPLE'S RULES

If the Bedouin are independent and make their own rules, who governs them and who decides what should happen? We have seen that the Bedouin sheikhs are men with more influence in the tribes than others, who can persuade people but not order them about. But they have no police and no army and do not rule like governments do. How does Bedouin society work?

The answer is that there are rules about hospitality and cooperation that all Bedouin observe. But also, Bedouin society is what anthropologists call a "segmentary" society. This means that when there are disputes, there is always someone a Bedouin can turn to for help. In the past there have been Bedouin feuds that have involved killing and looting. That happens less today because it attracts the attention of the police or the army.

But disputes are always controlled and end because neither side wants to do more harm or to suffer more. That is because a Bedouin can always call for help. If he is in dispute with his cousin, his brothers will help him. If he is in dispute with a more distant relation, his uncles and cousins will help him. And if he is fighting with someone outside his tribe, the whole tribe will help him. When it comes to dealings with the outside world, that is to say with you and me, all Bedouin will, if necessary, stick together against us.

That is the way the Bedouin of modern times have survived, and it is a way of life that isolated camel nomads have developed to ensure their survival through the centuries, over the four thousand years of their existence.

Three hundred years ago, an English writer named Thomas Hobbes wrote a famous book entitled *Leviathan* that said that if there was no government, everybody would try to kill everyone else, in order to steal their property or for other reasons. Hobbes did not know about the Bedouin, but their way of life proves him wrong.

▲   Bedouin people have their own rules for cooperation with each other and for hospitality toward visitors.

What Lies Ahead?

6

A THREATENED LIFE-STYLE

The Bedouin are threatened throughout the lands where they live. The climate of recent years has made the desert drier. Nobody yet knows if that change is permanent. But it has driven the Bedouin northward out of the desert and brought them into greater contact with settled people in towns and villages. That is a permanent social change, whether or not the weather returns to its earlier pattern.

In addition, the Bedouin are not immune to the economic problems of the world. The prices the Bedouin get for the goods they are able to trade are falling, and the loss of income affects their way of life.

A third factor that is threatening the Bedouin is that governments in the Arab countries where they live would like to see them settled because they see them as a disturbing influence. They have no fixed addresses, they seldom pay taxes, and they try to avoid government regulations, all of which government officials dislike.

The Arabs know that an important part of their culture has sprung from the desert roots of the Bedouin. They have an idealized notion of Bedouin life, but they often do not like the

▲ A Bedouin man, living next to a settled area, will still keep camels if possible.

◀ With changes in the climate making the desert drier, the sands are forever moving to cover the more fertile land. This means that each year, there is less land both for farming and for grazing animals.

Bedouin in practice. When townspeople in Arab countries meet the Bedouin, they think the Bedouin are dirty and dishonest, or even possibly dangerous. At the same time, they look down on the Bedouin for being, as the townspeople think, a little simple, while they also believe they are very crafty.

For all these reasons, the Bedouin are endangered. How many Bedouin there are left in the world is hard to estimate, but it may be less than three million. They keep alive a way of life that has endured for many centuries, and once they have disappeared that way of life will be gone forever.

ASSIMILATION?

The question arises in a country where there are Bedouin whether it is the government's responsibility to make their lives easier by helping them to continue their Bedouin customs by releasing them from taxation or possibly even offering them subsidies. Or should it try to settle the Bedouin, turn them into farmers, and encourage them to accept education that will help them to find jobs?

Undoubtedly, the second alternative will give Bedouin families a higher standard of living and perhaps mean that their children will be able to lead different lives. But it will do so at the cost of destroying an ancient and honorable way of life which is greatly treasured by those men and

Pride

Bedouin life is not necessarily the most profitable existence that these people could have, but it is the life to which they have been brought up, and it is a way of living of which Bedouin men and women are very proud. Some of its essential features are no longer really economically viable. There is little profit to be made from camel herding today, but the Bedouin men continue with it because they love the life and the animals. The sale of carpets is no longer so profitable and scarcely supplies the cash the Bedouin need to buy the things they cannot make themselves, but the women continue to make the carpets because they are proud of their skill.

▼ The nomadic way of life is hard but worth preserving.

women who presently live it.

Some countries are more eager to settle the Bedouin than others. But throughout the Arab world, there is a tendency to favor policies that will settle the Bedouin and bring them more into line with modern society.

A WORTHWHILE AIM

If the Bedouin were settled, there would no longer be living examples of one of the bravest and most ingenious ways men and women have devised to cope with a hostile environment. That in itself would be a tragedy. In addition, human society needs to flourish in all its variety. Just as it diminishes the natural world when a species becomes extinct, the world of human beings becomes poorer when one of the world's cultures ceases to exist. To find ways of allowing the Bedouin to continue to roam the desert would be an aim worth achieving.

Glossary

Aquifer   An underground channel or reservoir of water, often very far below the ground and frequently present even in places that look like deserts.

Bedouin   An English word that comes from the Arabic word for Bedouin, "Bedu."

Breadwinner   Someone who works to support his or her family.

Climate   What the weather is like in a country over a long time. The climate of Tunisia is hot and dry, even though there are some rainy days.

Delta   In Greek the letter *D* is called *delta*. The capital letter is like a triangle standing on its base: Δ. This is the shape of the marshy triangular area that is often found at a river's mouth, where it runs into the sea, and so such an area is called a delta.

Economy/economic   The economy means everything to do with how we produce things and consume them, and how we make and spend money. The word *economic* means anything to do with the economy.

Hashemite   A member of the Bani Hashem tribe of southern Arabia. It is used today to refer to the particular family from which King Hussein of Jordan is descended. King Hussein's great grandfather, Hussein Ibn Ali, was the governor of Mecca in 1915, and, after World War I, his son Faisal became king of Iraq, while another son, Abdullah, became king of Jordan.

Hospitality   Welcoming guests and showing generosity and kindness to them.

Islam   The religion of Muslims, founded by Muhammad, whom the Muslims believe was a prophet. The holy book of Islam is the Koran, which Muslims believe was revealed to Muhammad by God.

Leviathan   A gigantic sea creature mentioned in the Bible. Thomas Hobbes used the word to mean a whole country, or state, in a book he wrote about the idea of government, published in 1651. It is still read seriously today, more than 300 years later.

Maghreb   What the Arabs call the Arab countries in the west, from Libya to Morocco. *Maghreb* means "the place where the sun sets" in Arabic. Arabs sometimes call the eastern Arab countries the *Mashriq* which means "the place where the sun rises."

Mythological   Something connected with the stories or myths that people believe in or at least tell to each other.

Nationality   The nation a person belongs to as a citizen. So, a Bedouin may be Tunisian, or Syrian or another Arab nationality, while people who live in the U.S. are mostly American. But many people today live in one country and have the nationality of another.

Nomad/nomadism   Someone who travels from place to place as a way of life and does not have a fixed home. *Nomadism* means being a nomad. Nomads do not move constantly and may stay in the same place for months or years, but they are always able to move away. Bedouins are nomads.

Ottoman   The Ottoman Empire is the name given to the Turkish empire that ruled the Arab countries of the Middle East for five hundred years, until the end of World War I in 1918, when Arab countries became independent.

Peninsula   An area of land mainly surrounded by sea and joined only by a relatively narrow link to the land nearby. Saudi Arabia is one of the countries of the Arabian Peninsula.

Pilgrimage A journey people make to a holy place. For Muslims, the holiest pilgrimage is the one to Mecca, the birthplace of the prophet Muhammad and the spiritual center of Islam. It takes place once each year, and every Muslim should make it at least once during his or her lifetime.

Sahel The semidesert area that is found at the edge of the real desert. "Sahel" in Arabic means "seashore." When people say *sahel* about the edge of the desert, they are thinking poetically of it as a sea of sand.

Segmentary Divided into parts, or segments. The segments that a society may be divided into are segments of families, clans, or tribes.

Tribe A group of people who share a common descent from the same ancestors, or who believe they do, who usually live close to each other and have a similar way of life.

Ululation A special way of crying out that Arab women are able to do, especially at celebrations. Try shouting "eeee" in a very high voice, with your mouth wide open, and wagging your tongue from side to side at the same time. It is difficult to do, but you can get recordings of what it should sound like.

Unemployment The situation where some people do not have jobs and cannot earn money.

Veterinarian/vet A doctor who looks after animals is called a "veterinarian" or "vet."

Further Reading

Alotaibi. *Bedouin: Nomads of the Desert*. Rourke, 1990

Baker, Lucy. *Life in the Deserts*. Watts, 1990

Chicago Zoological Society, ed. *Desert Communities*. Chicago Zoological Society, 1986

Curumbhoy, Nayana. *Living in Deserts*. Watts, 1987

Lerner Publications, Department of Geography Staff. *Syria in Pictures*. Lerner, 1990

McLeish, Ewan. *Spread of Deserts*. Steck-Vaughn, 1990

Moore, Randy and Vodopich, Darrell. *Deserts*. Enslow Publishers, 1991

Further Information

Middle East Institute
1761 N Street, NW
Washington, DC 20036

Middle East Research and Information Project
Suite 119
1500 Massachussetts Avenue, NW
Washington, DC 20005

Index

*Numbers in **bold** refer to pictures as well as text.*